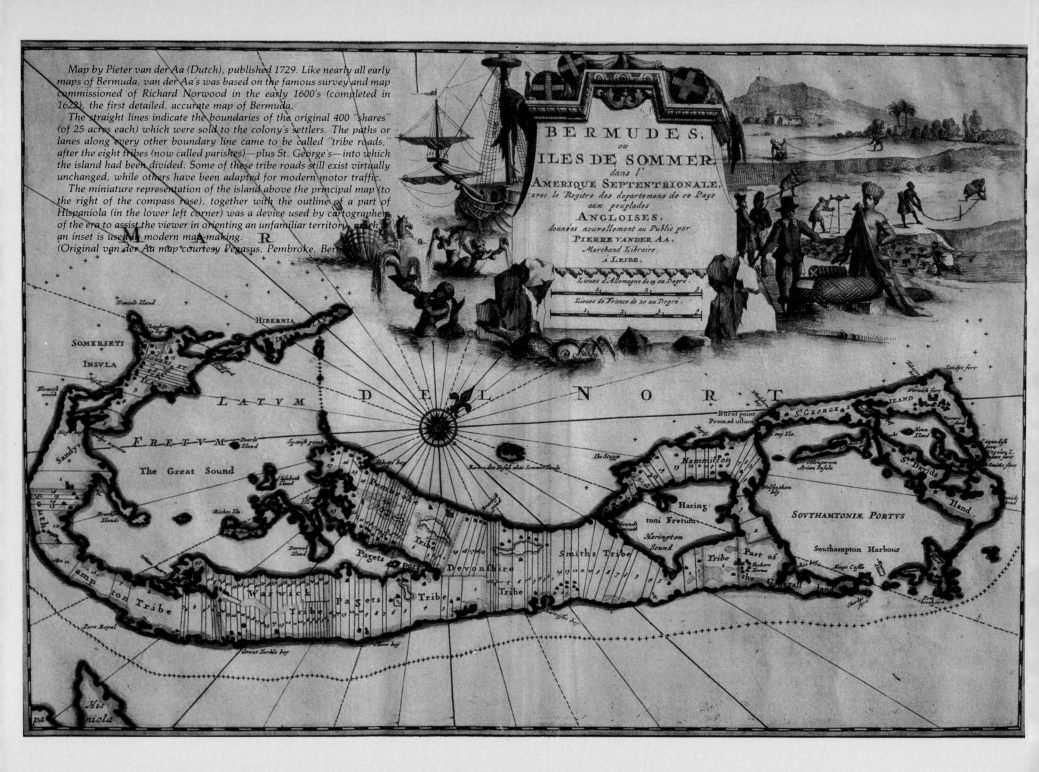

Map by Pieter van der Aa (Dutch), published 1729. Like nearly all early maps of Bermuda, van der Aa's was based on the famous survey and map commissioned of Richard Norwood in the early 1600's (completed in 1622), the first detailed, accurate map of Bermuda.

The straight lines indicate the boundaries of the original 400 "shares" (of 25 acres each) which were sold to the colony's settlers. The paths or lanes along every other boundary line came to be called "tribe roads," after the eight tribes (now called parishes)—plus St. George's—into which the island had been divided. Some of these tribe roads still exist virtually unchanged, while others have been adapted for modern motor traffic.

The miniature representation of the island above the principal map (to the right of the compass rose), together with the outline of a part of Hispaniola (in the lower left corner) was a device used by cartographers of the era to assist the viewer in orienting an unfamiliar territory, much as an inset is used in modern map-making.

(Original van der Aa map courtesy Pegasus, Pembroke, Bermuda)

For Martha,
who has always
thought they were
good enough

Though we travel the world over
to find the beautiful,
we must carry it with us
or find it not.

—*Ralph Waldo Emerson*

A young Bermudian in an old Bermudian setting, five-year old Tomeak Lang surveys the passing scene on one of St. George's winding lanes. The "push-out" blinds shading the window have been a fixture of the island's architecture for generations, for early settlers soon learned their value in keeping out summer sun and showers while letting in cooling breezes.

The history of this, the oldest of Britain's remaining colonies, has been a similar story writ larger: a story of a people shaping, and in turn being formed by, a tiny, special world in the midst of the vast Atlantic.

Images of Bermuda

Text and photographs by
Roger LaBrucherie

Imágenes Press

A ferry bound for the Warwick shore cuts the sunset-colored surface of Hamilton Harbour.

Foreword

As with my two previous books, in what has become a series of Images, Images of Bermuda is an attempt to capture the essence of a place and its people, primarily for the reader who has had only a relatively brief time to spend there.

From the time I first lived abroad, in the late 1960's, I have noticed that a newcomer's perception of a new land evolves gradually from one of great fascination (coupled with considerable ignorance), to one of near-total familiarity (coupled with becoming blasé to the differences that make every place and its people unique and potentially fascinating). Somewhere in between, I think, there is a period when understanding begins but the sense of wonder has not yet been lost. It is that perspective which I have always aspired to bring to my portrayal of a country.

Coupled with that aspiration is the belief that the modern tourist seeks to carry home more about the place he has visited than a series of post-card images. Hopefully he seeks as well some understanding of the people that make each culture unique. With Bermuda such a portrayal may be more difficult than in many places, for Bermuda is, of course, to a great extent "geared" for tourism. As Mrs. Terry Tucker, Bermuda's noted historian, has pointed out, even the island's history is sometimes popularized to make for a more saleable "product."

And yet Bermuda is more, much more, than the "country as Disneyland" a friend of mine once described her as being. I had what I believe was the great good fortune of first knowing Bermuda in winter, the "off" season, when the pace slows, the island is less full of visitors, and Bermuda returns to her people. Then the sidewalks of Hamilton throng with people in tweeds and woolen scarves, and even a visitor such as myself is repeatedly greeted by passersby, in the small-town tradition which continues to make Bermuda such a delight in a world of generalized aloofness.

Seeing Bermuda for the first time in the off season helped me see her as a complete island-nation (for, despite her formal colonial status, nearly all Bermudians think of their land as an independent country, as indeed she is in nearly all but name) with a distinct culture, and with a people who accept—indeed, insist upon—responsibility for, and who aggressively seek solutions to, their own problems. If some visitors confuse the island with a magic kingdom, all the more reason Bermudians should have a feeling of self-satisfaction with the way they have managed their domain.

No book, I think, which hopes to convey a fairly complete portrait of Bermuda can ignore those aspects which make her so attractive to the tourist; and yet, my heart is with that Bermuda of the slower pace, the occasional cold and rainy days, the small-town greeting . . . I hope Images of Bermuda will convey a bit of that Bermuda as well to those who come to her primarily for her fabled sun, sand, and sea.

Geneva, August, 1980

Beginnings

*I*ts 16th-Century inscription joined by scores of more recent ones, Spanish Rock*, perched on a cliff overlooking the Atlantic near Spittal Pond, bears witness to a visitor to Bermuda—almost certainly Spanish or Portuguese—whose identity has been lost to time. The date "1543" and uncertain initials are all the record we have of his visit, but the "bones" of scores of shipwrecks lying among the reef-studded shallow waters surrounding Bermuda are ample proof that many more 16th-Century Iberians came to know Bermuda the hard way. It was a better (or luckier?) seaman, however, the Spaniard Juan Bermúdez, whom history records as the island's discoverer. He sighted, but apparently did not land on, Bermuda in the early 1500's (perhaps 1503, and almost certainly by 1509), and to him fell the honor of the island's name. (Not without some dispute, however: the English, wanting to honor Sir George Somers, the man who had been vital to the very survival of Bermuda's first English residents, gave the name Somers' Island to the colony. Though the Spaniard has won out in popular parlance, certain of Bermuda's formal documents to this day carry both names.)

Those scattered, and mostly unfortunate, Iberian contacts during the 1500's were the first human contacts with Bermuda which history records. Because the conquistadores were primarily in search of precious metals and gems, of which Bermuda was bereft, the island and its extensive reefs were seen primarily as a navigational hazard on the route home from the New World—undoubtedly a major factor in causing the Spanish to dub the island "La Isla de Demonios" (Island of the Devils). Small wonder, then, that they gave Bermuda a wide berth, and that Bermuda remained uninhabited throughout the 16th Century.

---

*Centuries of human and natural wear and tear at the rock's inscription recently led to its being capped with a bronze tablet replica.

As though sailing into the storm that brought her to grief—and salvation—on the reefs of Bermuda, the Sea Venture rides the winds atop Hamilton's City Hall (**opposite**). The flagship of a supply fleet bound for Jamestown, England's fledgeling colony in Virginia, in 1609, the Sea Venture had been separated from her sister ships and buffeted for days by gale-force winds when, near sinking, land was sighted. Now the reefs, long a deadly menace to Spanish and Portuguese ships homeward bound from their New World colonies, proved kinder to the English vessel, holding her tight in their grip until the storm subsided. The ship was a loss, but passengers and cargo made it safely to shore. The date was July 28, 1609, and Bermuda has been continuously inhabited ever since.

The castaways would spend ten months on the island, building a pair of small vessels to take them on to America. (One of those ships, the Deliverance, is replicated on Ordnance Island, off St. George. The account of the shipwreck and the survivors' sojourn is thought to have inspired Shakespeare's play, The Tempest, which was first performed in 1611.) Two years later, the survivors' glowing accounts of the island would persuade the Virginia Company of London* to establish a colony in Bermuda as well.

Thus, in July of 1612 sixty English colonists, the first of many hundreds to be sent out by the company in the following years, landed at the island's eastern end and founded a settlement, which they named St. George. Their mission was to produce profits for the company, supposedly to be found in pearls, whale-oil, farm products (especially sugar and tobacco), and in ambergris—a substance secreted by sperm whales and highly valued in perfume-making.

They found the island naturally bountiful: in addition to wild hogs (which the Spanish had loosed on the island to provide a food supply for shipwrecks), there were turtles, fish, and a nearly-tame sea-bird, the cahow, as plentiful sources of meat, and the mild climate would permit year-round vegetable cultivation. It would not be long, moreover, before Bermudians would see a profit potential in the fate which had befallen the Sea Venture, and sometimes give fate a helping hand. Telescope to his eye, decoy bonfire lit, a "wrecker" (**this page**) searches the horizon for sign of sail—just so did some less-scrupulous Bermudians seek to lure unwary night-sailing sea captains in search of safe harbour onto Bermuda's uncharted reefs. (To then loot the ship of its cargo.) Though perhaps larger in legend than in actual history, the practice, together with more-common privateering (and some outright piracy), helped see Bermuda through its early lean years.

And lean years there would be, for before many years had passed the island's long-stored natural bounty would be depleted, and the colonists, many of whom had been less than keen on farming to begin with, would discover that Bermuda was ill-suited for sugar and tobacco production. Indeed, the poor showing of the colony as a commercial venture would lead to constant squabbles between the colonists and the sponsoring company, and to the eventual transfer (in 1684) of the colony's charter from the company to the Crown.** But in 1612 these developments were still far in the future; the adventurous spirits who launched the colony were undoubtedly more taken with its possibilities than with whatever drawbacks might eventually come to light.

---

*In 1615 the colony was passed to the related Somers Island Company.
**The term "Crown Colony" is inaccurate in Bermuda's case, however, for the island's settlers had acquired the right of self-government during the company's tenure, and this right was never surrendered.

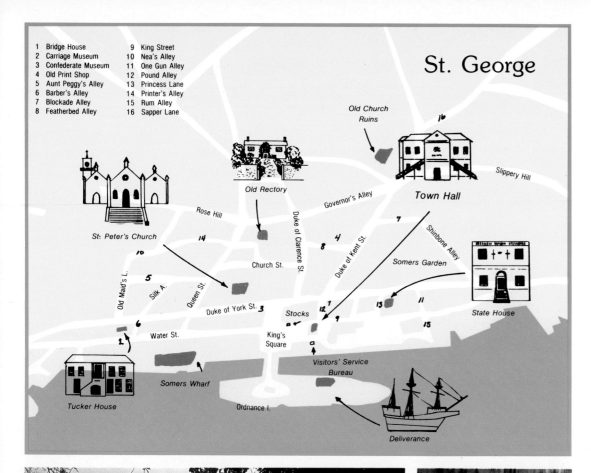

St. George

1 Bridge House
2 Carriage Museum
3 Confederate Museum
4 Old Print Shop
5 Aunt Peggy's Alley
6 Barber's Alley
7 Blockade Alley
8 Featherbed Alley
9 King Street
10 Nea's Alley
11 One Gun Alley
12 Pound Alley
13 Princess Lane
14 Printer's Alley
15 Rum Alley
16 Sapper Lane

Old Church Ruins

Town Hall

Slippery Hill

Old Rectory

Governor's Alley

Rose Hill

Duke of Clarence St.

Shinbone Alley

St. Peter's Church

Somers Garden

Church St.

Duke of Kent St.

Old Maid's L.

Silk A.

Queen St.

Duke of York St.

Stocks

King's Square

State House

Water St.

Somers Wharf

Ordnance I.

Visitors' Service Bureau

Tucker House

Deliverance

OLD RECTORY

*L*ocated at the island's eastern extreme, on an excellent harbour and, above all, near the sole break in the encircling reefs permitting safe entry for deep-draft ships, it was natural that St. George grew to become the commercial and governmental "center" of the island. In fact, from the colony's founding, in 1612, until the establishment of Hamilton nearly 200 years later, St. George was Bermuda's only town.

Thus St. George became a concentration of some of the colony's oldest structures, such as the Old State House (the island's first stone building, built in the 1620's), the Old Globe Hotel (c. 1698), the Tucker House (c. 1711), and the Old Rectory (c. 1705, **this page**), which takes its name from its one-time service as residence for the rector of the parish church of St. George's. The early pattern of narrow, twisting streets (with names like "One Gun Alley," "Old Maid's Lane," and "Featherbed Alley") leading to wharf-side King's Square, and buildings dating from the colony's first centuries characterize St. George to this day (see aerial view, **opposite**). In fact, it is probable that an 18th-Century St. Georgian, if transported to the present, would feel very much at home in St. George, so little has it changed.

Plugged and capped keyholes in the cedar door of the Old Rectory (**this page**), bear witness to changes in ownership of the house over the years. (Today used as a private residence, the structure is the property of the Bermuda National Trust, an organization dedicated to the preservation of the Bermudian heritage.)

*J*ewel of St. George, pride of the colony, St. Peter's Church (**opposite,** in a night view), has stood at the center of the island's oldest community, and at the heart of her people's affections, since the founding of St. George in 1612. (The present structure dates from 1713, although much altered and added to over the years; a complete restoration, undertaken with the view of preserving the authenticity of the building, was completed in the early 1950's).

An interior view (**this page**), looks eastward toward the red cedar altar, which, according to tradition, dates from 1612. A brass ewer glistens in a 15th-Century stone font (foreground), brought from England by the colony's earliest settlers.

St. Peter's today lays claim to being the oldest continuously-used Anglican church in the Western Hemisphere; it has, throughout its history, however, served the community for non-religious functions as well: the first meetings of Parliament were held there, as were early criminal trials. In 1970 Prince Charles there read the Throne Speech to an assemblage of dignitaries gathered to commemorate the 350th Anniversary of Bermuda's Parliament.

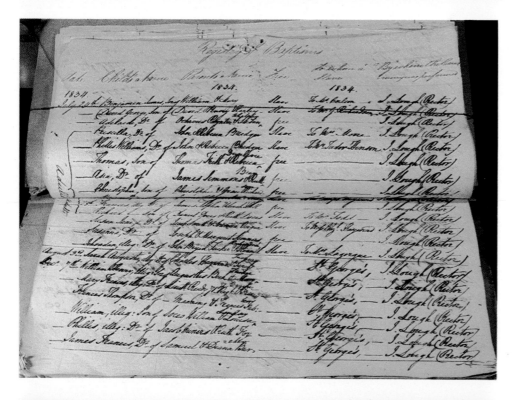

Vivid record of a shadowed past, the historic Baptismal Registry of St. Peter's Church **(upper left)**, shows the matter-of-fact way in which the end of slavery in Bermuda was accepted by the Anglican Church, at least: after emancipation, which occurred August 1, 1834, the registry simply ceases to indicate the status ("free" versus "slave") of the child—henceforth, all were free.

It goes without saying that, after two centuries of slavery, the social, economic, and human adjustments to the change were far more difficult and long-lasting. It has been well argued that conditions under Bermuda's small-scale slavery may have been less arduous than those on large American and West Indian plantations; but the history of 18th-Century slave rebellions is nonetheless unmistakable evidence of the position the slaves endured.

How then, given this history, have Bermudians managed to evolve a society in which all traces of racism and rancor over past injustices are absent? The answer is quite simple: they have not. Only a Pollyanna would argue that no such traces remain. (In fact, the colony experienced serious civil disturbances—largely racial in origin—during the late 1960's and in the 1970's.) But the following is equally clear: the vast majority of Bermudians are at ease in one another's company, white or black, and they are committed to making their island one in which those traces will steadily and completely disappear.

They are already well along that road. I think they will arrive.

* * *

Perhaps no one has contributed more to the modern widespread knowledge of Bermuda's beginnings—and to an understanding of her present—than has author-historian Terry Tucker, posed here in the museum of the Bermuda Historical Society **(lower left)**. (I first met her—as has no doubt many another visiting writer in search of answers to Bermuda's puzzles—behind her desk at the Bermuda Library, clipping and filing newspaper articles for the reference section. I was as captivated by her lively personality and wit as I had been earlier by her lucid writing.)

Her numerous books and articles, plus her ever-readiness to lend a hand or a thoughtful observation—to researchers in Bermudian history, have made her, in the words of one admirer, "a national treasure of the first order."

A younger student of Bermudian history—a primary-four pupil at the St. George's Preparatory School—steals a moment from the classroom assignment to smile into the camera (**upper right**).

* * *

A drawing created by one of her younger school-mates at the primary two level (**lower right**) presents a graphic explanation of Bermuda's geologic origin. Capping the extinct volcano which forms Bermuda's foundation—long ago worn away to a height below today's shore line—is a layer of aeolian limestone (composed chiefly of cemented sand and shell particles) several hundred feet thick which has eroded to its present hilly aspect. As anyone who has seen the island from the air knows (see aerial photograph, end of chapter), the part of Bermuda showing above water covers only a small part of that volcanic submarine platform: an area perhaps ten times as large lies just below the surface. Much of that submerged platform is dotted with the reefs which completely surround the island. Though often referred to as "coral reefs," they are, in fact, primarily of a calcareous algae structure. (Bermuda is, thanks to the warming Gulf Stream, the most northerly point on the globe where reef-building coral is found, but coral composes only a small fraction of the reef material.)

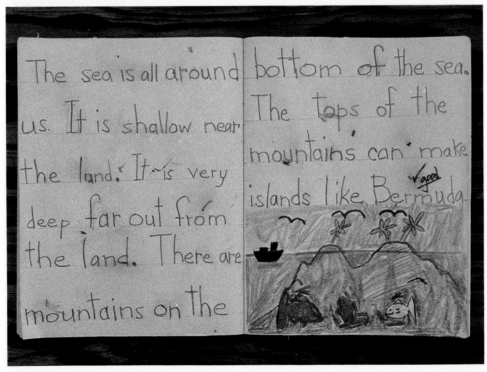

The sea is all around us. It is shallow near the land. It is very deep far out from the land. There are mountains on the bottom of the sea. The tops of the mountains can make islands like Bermuda.

Though St. George was for nearly two centuries Bermuda's only town, the rest of the colony hardly remained uninhabited, for settlers quickly spread out over the nine parishes, which (except for St. George's, which was technically not a parish*) had been named for the principal shareholders of the Somers Island Company. There they established small farms and built rustic dwellings, first of wattle-and-daub, or perhaps cedar, and almost certainly roofed with thatch from the indigenous palmetto. Later, when the danger posed by hurricanes was understood and the islanders grew more prosperous, these rude structures would be replaced by the simple houses of limestone construction which came to be known (as they are today) as the "Bermuda cottage."

Somerset, in Sandys Parish at the western end of the island, is perhaps the area where the greatest concentration of these historic farm cottages is still found—houses such as "Belfield" (**this page**), "Shrewsbury," and "Virginia Cottage"—for Somerset long remained essentially a rural area and, until the arrival of motor vehicles, remote from the changes which inevitably altered the character of the central parishes.

It would not be until the age of air travel, of course, that a scene like the one opposite would be witnessed, but one can well imagine that had an early Bermudian had this vantage point, he would have been shocked by the tiny dimensions of his "world." As generations of later-comers have discovered, Bermuda's rolling topography and thick vegetation deceive the eye, making it appear far larger than its scant 21 square miles.

In this view, looking southwesterly**, St. George's Island (right) and St. David's Island dominate the foreground (an arm of St. David's juts into Castle Harbour at the center of the picture), while beyond, the Main Island encircles Harrington Sound and curves around the Great Sound, leading to the "tip of the fishhook," consisting of Somerset, Watford, Boaz and Ireland Islands, at upper right.

---

*Nor, technically speaking, were the other eight, since originally the parishes were called "tribes"; the historic name lives on in the term "tribe roads," originally narrow lanes demarking the boundaries of the settlers' parcels of land.

**I am indebted to the Bermuda News Bureau, and to Mr. James Babineau, photographer, for the original of this aerial view. Although I have never before used another photographer's work in my books, I was simply unable to get a shot this good—but I am grateful to Wing Commander E.M. "Mo" Ware and his little float plane for helping me try.

The first two centuries of the colony's history—characterized by a boom-and-bust existence dependent on subsistence farming and the various sea trades (the latter made all the more uncertain as Bermuda's long-time trading partners, the American Colonies, broke with the mother country and thus became off-limits to Bermudian vessels)—gave way to a greater degree of economic stability beginning with the 19th Century.

*Though Bermudians—as Englishmen, but with close ties to the American Colonies dating from their founding—may have been divided over the issue of American independence, there could be no denying the economic benefit which came to Bermuda when her own strategic value to England was magnified by the loss of the American outposts. In 1810 construction began on a complex, vast for the time, on Ireland Island, the Royal Navy Dockyard (**this page**, in an aerial view looking southward). Construction and manning of the facility would provide Bermuda with a major source of jobs and income—hence economic stability—until the mid-20th Century, when Britain's changing economic and strategic position would bring another change: the decommissioning of the yard. Thus would come to an end Bermuda's century and a half as Britain's "Gibraltar of the West."*

Though its strategic role is a thing of the past, the Dockyard's buildings remain as a reminder of that era. Today they house various commercial and governmental entities, as well as the Bermuda Maritime Museum, which houses an excellent collection portraying Bermuda's long involvement with the sea.

Heritage

B lasé to a scene repeated hundreds of times during a busy tourist day, a St. Georgian turns a blind eye to the antics of visitors posing in the stocks in King's Square **(this page).** Though quaint today, these instruments of punishment must have put a chill in many a soul in the early days of the colony, when they were used for a more serious purpose. Together with the ducking stool and other more painful consequences (which included branding, whipping, and hanging), the punishments often seem harsh to the modern eye—especially when considered alongside their corresponding offenses. It was, it goes without saying, a different era, a time when the colony's very survival might hinge on the maintenance of a strict discipline, for the colony more than once found itself on the brink of starvation in its early years.

Happily, other, less distasteful, reminders of the island's early days have survived as well; in fact, some of them are downright tasty: "As many recipes as there are Bermudian cooks," runs the refrain when one asks the ingredients of cassava pie, Bermuda's traditional Christmas fare. As often as not the recipe is handed down from mother to daughter or granddaughter—and the traditional way requires the old bake oven adjoining the fireplace, still to be found in a few old cottages.

"There were various ways of testing the oven for the right temperature before modern stoves came along," Mrs. Barbara Henry told me. "The usual way was to put an egg shell in—if it turned brown, the temperature was hot enough—about 400 degrees. But my grandmother's cook had a very unusual way: she'd stick her head in the oven to test it!"

Mrs. Henry's ingredients, laid out on a rustic table in her early 18th-Century cottage, Stamp House **(opposite):** ground cassava root, chicken, milk, eggs, sugar, nutmeg, and salt. (Many cooks would add pork and beef as well.)

Though primarily British in its roots, Bermuda's culture springs from many outside sources—Africa, the West Indies, North America, most recently—and from Bermuda herself, as the island's conditions have subtly shaped and transformed foreign traditions and created her own. Just how much foreign, how much local, influence is contained in the dance and costume of the gombeys ("gum-bays") is difficult to say. A similar custom in many of the islands of the Caribbean points irrefutably to an African origin, imported via the slave ships—while variations in costume, often mimicking local convention (such as the bobby's black helmet), reveal the indigenous contribution.

Whatever the source, the gombeys' whirling dance, to the accompaniment of drums and fife, has been on the scene—especially on traditional holidays such as New Year's, Easter Monday, and Boxing Day (December 26)—for time immemorial in Bermuda.

Opposing counsel pause during a court recess to pose for the camera (**opposite**). Their robes and wigs, descendants of 17th-Century English tradition, indicate that their case is being heard in the Supreme Court chamber, (where this photograph was taken), a tribunal of both original and appellate jurisdiction in Bermuda. (Matters of a less serious nature, such as traffic violations, are heard in one of the Magistrate's Courts.) Bermuda's body of law is based on its Constitution (extensively amended and first taking written form in 1968), as well as on English Common Law.

A tradition of civility and mutual respect (perhaps aided by her small size) has kept Bermuda remarkably crime-free, although in that sense, as in many others, Bermuda—as she loses her physical and cultural isolation—is coming to resemble the outside world. (During my stay in Bermuda a referee was the target of bottles thrown during a match by irate soccer fans, an event viewed with shock by many who had long assumed Bermuda to be exempt from such behavior. "Of course these things will happen," one elderly lady confided. "We can hardly expect to take the benefits of the modern world without getting some of the bad too. But sometimes I wonder, darlin', if we really come out ahead.")

The House of Assembly Chamber their schoolroom-for-a-day (**this page**), a class of primary-four youngsters learn the workings of Parliament from a first-hand observer, the chamber's Sergeant-at-Arms. Portraits of King George III and his Queen Charlotte adorn the wall behind the Speaker's chair; the presence of the silver Mace indicates that the "House" is in session.

The youngsters have a proud history to contemplate: the Parliament first convened in 1620, thus making it the Commonwealth's oldest representative government outside the British Isles. The system of government has undergone a steady evolution since its inception, most notably in the general extension of the franchise and the removal of its property-ownership requirement, and in the expansion of the areas over which Bermudians exercise local control.

Under the 1968 Constitution the House of Assembly (composed of 40 members), and the Legislative Council (11 members) comprise the Legislature. The Governor, appointed by the British Head of State (presently Queen Elizabeth II), is responsible for external affairs, internal security, and defence. The remaining Executive functions are the responsibility of the Premier (the leader of the majority party) and the Cabinet which he appoints.

The Sessions House, which houses both the Assembly Chamber and the chambers of the Supreme Court, dates from the early 1800's, when the Capital was transferred to Hamilton from St. George. The distinctive southern towers and verandah were added in 1887, to commemorate Queen Victoria's Jubilee. (See "Hamilton" for an exterior view of the Sessions House.)

*T*he colony's Governor repeats an annual ceremony as he reviews military units drawn up for inspection on Front Street (**opposite**) in commemoration of the Queen's Birthday, which is celebrated officially in mid-June. Such occasions, with their traditional pomp, serve to remind Bermudians of their historic and continuing relationship with Britain, dating back nearly four centuries.

It has been a relationship which has evolved with changing conditions and ideas: as has been noted, Bermudians have had, since the earliest days of the colony, the right to enact local laws (always with the proviso that they not conflict with British law, which took precedence), but the Governor, representing the Crown, historically had the most powerful voice in island affairs. As elsewhere, the trend has been to greater local self-rule, and while it would be an exaggeration to say that the Governor's role today is purely a ceremonial one, Bermuda is now essentially self-governing via its elected government.

Full independence has been, and no doubt will continue to be, debated among Bermudians. As with other colonies, Britain has indicated her willingness to accept the decision of the local majority on the matter—but it is impossible to predict which road Bermuda will choose to follow. Clearly a great many Bermudians, like this old trouper (**this page**) surveying the Queen's Birthday festivities, retain a deep pride in the island's British heritage—a pride which will weigh heavily in that choice, whatever it may be.

*B*raced at attention, drummer Clayton DeRosa of the Bermuda Regiment's Band awaits inspection before a Rendezvous Season performance in King's Square, St. George **(opposite)**. Though usually seen by the visitor in a purely ceremonial role, the Regiment is in fact, in its principal capacity, the island's primary external defence force. (Bermuda is, of course, a part of the British Commonwealth, and as such a participant in its defence system.)

The Regiment was formally constituted in 1965, growing out of two historic units—the Bermuda Rifles and the Bermuda Militia Artillery—which had seen service in both World Wars. Today all young Bermudian males register for military service, and the Regiment is composed of conscripts from that pool as well as volunteers, both male and female. A squad of corporals **(this page)** crouch in readiness as they prepare to demonstrate a training exercise to new recruits assembled on the beach near Warwick Camp, the Regimental Headquarters.

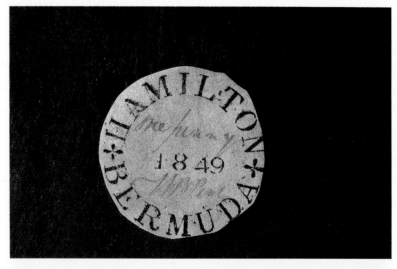

*C*rossroads of Hamilton, the Perot Post Office (**opposite**, *an interior view*) is as much social center as it is working post office, for it seems there is seldom a moment when a couple of friends are not catching up on the latest news and gossip. Unlike St. George's, Hamilton's aspect has changed greatly since its late 18th-Century beginnings; the skyline alters inexhorably under the pressure for more space from commercial, business, and governmental interests. All the more reason, then, that Bermudians regard the Perot Post Office with such fondness, for it represents the Hamilton of the mid-1800's, when the city had a more intimate air. (Bermudians have adopted the habits of bigger places, like using their cars and mo-peds to go across town.)

The building dates from the 1840's, when the city post-master, William Perot, built the structure to serve as both post office and dwelling. (The adjacent park and building housing the Library, Archives and Historical Society Museum all formed part of Perot's property, "Par-la-Ville.")

But Mr. Perot was to leave an even more-renowned reminder of his 40-plus years as Hamilton's postmaster: in 1848 he began combining his postal cancellation stamp, his signature, and the words "one penny" on sheets of paper—thereby creating Bermuda's first postage stamps. Of the doubtless thousands of such stamps created (Perot continued his practice until the mid-1860's, when Bermuda's first printed stamps made their appearance), only seventeen are known to still exist. In 1980 a specimen like the one pictured here (**this page, upper left**), sold at auction for £70,000 (about $170,000 at 1980 exchange rates).

A more familiar sight, red British-style postboxes, add splashes of colour to Bermuda's landscape (**this page, lower left**).

(Perot Stamp courtesy Baron Stig Leuhusen, Hamilton.)

M embers of the Council of the Bermuda National Trust pose (**opposite**) before its jewel, Verdmont, an historic Smith's Parish house which has remained virtually unaltered since its construction in the early 18th Century. (Though used as a private residence until its careful restoration and conversion to a museum in the 1950's, neither plumbing nor electricity have ever been added.)

Founded in 1970, the Bermuda National Trust today brings together over 2,000 Bermudians concerned at the loss of heritage—both natural and man-made—threatened by the pace of Bermuda's recent development.

"For too long we Bermudians were oblivious to the treasures we had around us," one Trust member told me. "A lot of beautiful old houses in Hamilton, for example, were lost to some very ill-considered office buildings. We cannot—nor do we seek to—save every old structure; but there are so many pressures for 'progress' that the full price of that progress is not always considered. We already have one of the highest living standards in the world—will Bermuda be better off, if, in search of an ever-higher one and more jobs, we end up looking like Miami Beach?"

In addition to restoring, preserving, and administering architectural treasures such as Verdmont, the Old Rectory, and "Springfield" (in Somerset), the Trust also owns protected natural habitats such as Spittal Pond, where a young Little Blue Heron seeks an early-morning meal (**this page, upper**).

The Trust has its headquarters in yet another architectural gem, "Waterville" (c. 1720, **this page, lower**), a gift to the Trust from the Trimingham family. (Located at the foot of Hamilton Harbour, Waterville also houses a delightful octogenarian, Miss Elsie Gosling, who can be seen regularly on the front steps of the house, feeding the flock of wild ducks who have adopted her as their mistress.)

With its proud history in the piloting trade, it is no wonder that to this day St. David's Island continues to supply many of the pilots and men who crew the pilot boats—men such as Skipper Headley Millett and Engineer James Foggo (right and left, respectively, in the picture **opposite**), of the pilot boat St. Brendan, who have been together in the trade since their teens. Like nearly all their fellow islanders, they have a reputation for sturdiness and independence of spirit (perhaps due to an infusion of blood of Mahican Indians from America, who formed a part of the early slave population) which is almost legendary in Bermuda—and since they are both well into their seventies, and show no inclination to retire anytime soon, it seems a reputation well earned.

Though the linking, in the 1930's, of St. David's to the remainder of Bermuda by bridge ended forever St. David's historic physical isolation, there is no denying that St. David's continues to be a world apart. It is perhaps, as one Bermudian told me, a difference more easily felt than seen, although some differences come to the eye as well: nowhere else are so many wooden houses still standing; nowhere else does the motor vehicle—indeed, all the trappings of the 20th Century—seem so far away; nowhere else does the pace seem so measured (even the St. David's Islander's speech seems slower); but, above all, nowhere else has the sea remained so close to the center of life. (For all Hamilton's fine restaurants, a Bermudian will tell you, the finest seafood dinners are still to be found in the kitchens of St. David's Island.)

Thus a long-abandoned fishing boat (**this page, upper**) blends naturally with the surroundings and becomes a playground for neighborhood children; and a St. David's home would be incomplete without the mariner's old stand-by, the shark-oil barometer (**lower**)—the likelihood of bad weather ahead increasing as the cloudiness at the bottom of the bottle rises.

*B*ermuda was born of men and women who dared the sea; among her earliest settlers were sea-faring men; and England's ascent to great-power status had depended wholly on her domination of the seas—small wonder, then, that from the earliest days of her history Bermuda's settlers turned to the sea for their livelihoods and fortunes. Agricultural exploitation may have been high on the Somers Island Company's list of priorities, but few colonists shared that enthusiasm for the soil for very long. (Historian Terry Tucker recounts the shock of Governor William Reid at finding only two serviceable plows in the entire colony upon his arrival in 1839.)

The Bermudians' involvement in the sea (including privateering and wrecking) has been briefly noted in the first chapter. But the legitimate carrying trade was undoubtedly her greatest source of steady employment and revenue. Bermudian ships traveled the world over, earning both Bermudian sailors and shipbuilders an enviable reputation; but even the best Bermudian captains—as well as those less familiar with

Bermuda's waters—soon learned the dangers posed by the reefs encircling the island.

Thus it was natural that specialists—pilots, as they are called in maritime parlance—soon took over the task of guiding ships into St. George's Harbour; and since the hills of St. David's Island provided the best vantage points for sighting approaching ships, it was further natural that St. David's Islanders came to dominate the piloting trade. In an earlier time, before the arrival of small powered boats in the 20th Century, pilot "gigs" manned by six to eight oarsmen (such as that portrayed on a stamp issued in 1977, shown **this page**) would race to an approaching vessel; by tradition, the first to arrive got the job.

I accompanied a modern-day pilot, a veteran with more than 20 years of service, David Darrell, on a run as he guided the container ship Oleander on its weekly exit from Hamilton Harbour via Two Rock Passage, into the Great Sound, then along the North Shore, to the passage through the barrier reef, The Narrows, off St. George's Island. "This is the only place where large vessels can get in and out," he told me as we cleared The Narrows. "Just over there's Town Cut Channel, for St. George. Now, on a small ship like this one there's not much to it—plenty of clearance all around. It's on the big cruise ships where you earn your pay."

Our conversation was interrupted as the diesel-powered launch marked "Pilots" (as seen, **opposite**, approaching a cruise ship off the mouth of St. George's Harbour) pulled alongside to take us aboard and a rope ladder was dropped over Oleander's side. "It's sure a lot easier getting to and from the ships than it was in the old days," he commented once we had transferred to the pilot boat. "You know, those gigs would race fifty miles sometimes to get their pilot to the ship first. That's a lot of rowing!"

That historic tradition came to an end in 1929, when the government took over the service. As with many traditions, progress—this time in the form of modern ships and their insurers—had spelled the doom of the seat-of-the-pants, catch-as-catch-can piloting days.

Sea

*S*o, due to inclination and geography, Bermudians early turned to the sea for their prosperity—indeed, for their survival. It is a course which has influenced the island enormously throughout its history, for it has turned Bermuda toward the outside world and its developments, thus helping instill in its people a receptive and modern outlook, to a degree rare in an island people.

On a more prosaic level, it meant that Bermuda needed ships, and her shipwrights were soon fashioning the native cedar into some of the lightest, fastest ships afloat, the famed Bermuda sloops, and later, in the 1800's, the even faster clippers. (Ironically, the advent of the steam age in the early 19th Century, which numbered the days of the wooden ship, also spurred shipbuilders to produce the fastest clippers ever, in an effort to remain competitive.)

The heyday of shipbuilding is long past, of course, but Bermudian boatyards remain on the scene (**this page**). Today, however, the work is largely maintenance and repair, and the vessels, rather than the legendary clippers, are likely to be sleek racing sailboats, pleasurecraft, or working fishing boats.

Another reminder of the days when the island's prosperity depended on its working seamen lives on in Bermuda's famed fitted dinghies, descendants of working sailboats which once plied her waters. Probably no form of sailing engages Bermudians' attention and sense of history more than the dinghy races held in late spring and summer. Dinghy racers are a dedicated and tiny group (only five active dinghies still exist), but the results of their bi-weekly races (including the season opener held annually in May in St. George's Harbour, **opposite**) are followed closely by a wide audience.

I talked with Norman Roberts, Mayor of St. George, who skippered his Venture (a dinghy which he had, as a boy, helped his father build) to a victorious 1979 season: "These boats are strictly racing creatures—probably no boat in the world carries as much sail for its size. In dinghy racing it's often not a matter of where you place—it's whether you reach the finish line at all!" Indeed, the boats have so little freeboard that every race day I witnessed during the 1980 season included at least one sinking. In a tight race, it is common to see one or more crew members leap off the stern—giving the dinghy a push forward which may put it first across the finish line!

L ittle remains of Bermuda's one-time involvement with the sea trades, as Bermudians have turned "inland" for their fortunes; but one activity has gone on much as it has for centuries: Bermuda's working fishermen arise before dawn, go down to their boats, and make for their favorite fishing areas, often jealously guarded.

I joined Eugene Barnes and his son, Michael, on the Born Free one morning to fish the western reefs. "It may get a little windy, so we'll leave the nets and haul pots today," Mr. Barnes said, referring to the wire-mesh traps built in such a way that a fish can enter but not exit. We had soon crossed the Great Sound from the Born Free's mooring near Point Shares and passed under Watford Bridge to the extensive reefs to the west of Somerset Island. In a sea-scape without apparent markings, Mr. Barnes steered a steady course, then slowed the boat, stood, and studied the sea ahead. "There, Mike," he shouted, pointing to port. Michael threw a weighted rope into the water, pulled, and a plastic buoy broke the surface, an attached rope leading to the "pot" on the sea bed. Mr. Barnes hurried down from the bridge to help haul the 80-pound pot aboard. ("I wish I had a nickel for every time I've been up and down that ladder," he remarked ruefully later.)

The pattern was repeated over and over (**opposite**), as we roamed the reef, pulling in parrot fish, snapper, jacks, groupers, and once, one of Bermuda's highly-prized lobsters ("He goes back," said Michael, "out of season.") Before long I had asked the logical (landlubber's) questions: "Wouldn't it be a lot easier to find the buoys if they were on the surface?"

"Hah!" came the response. "We still have plenty of 'pirates' here in Bermuda." And secondly, after marvelling at Mr. Barnes' ability to find some forty-odd buoys without any surface reference whatever—for it was nearly impossible to see a buoy until nearly over it: "How do you know where they are?" To which came a reply requiring no words at all—just a finger pointing to the side of his head.

"Things have changed a lot since I started in this business," Mr. Barnes, who will soon leave the Born Free and the sea to Michael, told me. "Today we keep nearly everything we find in the pots—days gone by, you couldn't have given away half the fish we sell today for good money. Trouble is, you wonder if there'll be any fish left 20 years from now. They're getting harder and harder to find."

It's a hard life, but one Michael looks forward to—"Lots better than working in an office or a hotel—you're out in the air, you're your own boss, and on a good day I can make as much as I would in a week in an office job."

Like Michael, bearded Paul Lavigne (**this page**), whom I photographed as he sold the day's catch aboard The Rich One tied up along Front Street, prefers the rigours—and rewards—of the fisherman's life, and thus helps keep alive Bermuda's long tradition of turning to the sea.

The treasure fleets which carried bullion to Spain assembled each year at Havana, then took the usual route: northward on the Gulf Stream between Florida and the Bahamas, to catch the prevailing westerlies at about Latitude 32° N. The only obstacle in their path: Bermuda, with her extensive, deadly reefs. With the navigation and vessels of the day, many ships did not make it—among them, the San Pedro (wrecked in 1594, on the northern reef) and the San Antonio (1621, on the western).

Today a part of their treasure, including this ingot and a pair of gem-inlaid earrings (lower right), probably crafted in Colombia or Venezuela, make up the stunning collection of the Maritime Museum's Treasure House, housed at Dockyard. (The famed "Tucker Cross," found in the wreck of the San Pedro and reputedly the most valuable single object ever recovered from a Western Hemisphere wreck, was stolen from the collection sometime in the mid-1970's. Its whereabouts remain unknown.)

While Bermudians have plied the sea's surface since the colony's founding, the "last frontier" of the sea, to borrow a term, has awaited 20th-Century technology to become available to a wide audience. And it is, ironically, from that last, long-hidden province that have come reminders of man's earliest contacts with Bermuda—brief, unhappy contacts which led 16th-Century Spaniards to dub it "Isle of the Devils."

Symbolic of the treachery threatened by Bermuda's encircling reefs, as hypnotising today as when it was cast four centuries ago, a circular gold ingot flashes its brilliance in the Treasure House of the Bermuda Maritime Museum (upper left). On its face are seals indicating payment of the royal tax, the Roman numerals "XX" indicating, probably, the tally number, and the name stamp of the official assayer. The treasure's route to Bermuda was a circuitous one, but it almost certainly began high in the Andes, where Incas had mined it and then fashioned it into extraordinary works of art. The conquistadores, seeing in these masterpieces only symbols of a pagan and inferior culture, melted them into ingots such as this one for easy transport to Spain.

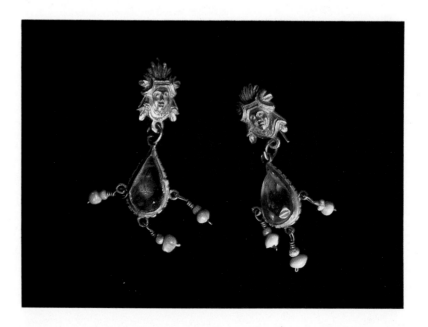

It is to Bermudian divers Harry Cox and Teddy Tucker that goes most of the credit for uncovering the spectacular treasures held by Bermuda's reefs; but even the amateur diver (as those seen, **previous page**, surfacing from a dive on the wreck of the Mary Celestia, a 19th-Century blockade runner) may find an old bottle or vase in one of Bermuda's scores of accessible wrecks, or simply discover that treasure awaiting any diver—the fantastic beauty of Bermuda's undersea world.

Considering the narrow confines of their increasingly-crowded island, it is hardly surprising that Bermudians continue to be irresistably lured by the wide-open freedom and solitude of the sea. After all, where else can a Bermudian legally go more than 20 miles per hour—or find a bit of solitude to share with a sunset?

The Onion Patch. . .

*C*onsidering how important has been the role of the sea in Bermuda's history, and Bermudians' traditional distaste for working the soil, it is ironic that in the latter 19th Century she gained a nickname reflecting the principal activity on the other side of her shoreline. Yet, the "Onion Patch" she became, as Bermuda onions (and potatoes, celery, carrots and tomatoes as well) became widely known and sought after in the northeastern United States.

As her historic economic mainstays connected with the sea began to decline in the mid-1800's, the vegetable trade grew to such scale that skilled farmworkers were in very short supply, especially after the emancipation of Bermuda's slaves in 1834 (for it was they who had performed the farm labor historically shunned by Bermudians). The solution was found in encouraging the immigration of Portuguese—already known for their agricultural skills—from the Azores. To this day farming, though no longer an export activity *, is dominated by Bermudians of Portuguese descent, although they have become prominent in commerce and the professions as well.

John Amaral, who immigrated from the Azores in the 1930's, shown here in his vegetable field in Paget (**this page, lower**), and his Bermudian-born son Gilbert run one of Hamilton's colorful "fruit stands" (**this page, upper**), a part of the Bermudian scene for as long as people can remember.

Another traditional aspect of Bermuda's agriculture, the horse-drawn plough, has all but disappeared from the scene, bowing to the higher productivity of the internal combustion engine. Gerald Woolridge, shown (**opposite**), working "Major" in his potato field, is one of those few Bermudian farmers who is not of

---

*The flow of farm products has now been completely reversed, since the tiny area available for farming—little more than a square mile all told—is far short of needs. As with nearly all products consumed in Bermuda, the great bulk of foodstuffs are imported. It is, in fact, the duty on imports—about 30% in most cases—which provides the greatest portion of government revenues, since the island has no personal or corporate income tax.

Portuguese ancestry. He came to the farmer's life in mid-career, after twenty-odd years in the restaurant trade. "I decided I was getting too old to put up with the foolishness you sometimes run into when people have had too much to drink," he told me. "This may pay a little less, but there's more to life than a few extra dollars." To residents of Warwick Parish he is a familiar sight on Middle Road, driving his wagon to or from a field, his Scottie "Gigi" invariably at his side.

Farming vegetables for export came to an end in the 1930's, when the U.S. Congress enacted a protective tariff. But by then the seeds of the 20th-Century industry on which Bermuda's unprecedented modern prosperity is founded had been sown: for the very steamers which regularly carried Bermuda's produce to New York and Boston had, before the end of the 19th Century, begun carrying a few snow-weary Yankees to the sun and sea of Bermuda. The island's tourist industry was born.

*I*t was perhaps not until that point that Bermudians began to appreciate that the lack of the natural resources on which a nation's prosperity is traditionally based (coal, mineral deposits, and water power, for example) was, in Bermuda's case, among her principal assets, for their absence meant that Bermuda had never undergone the industrial development which almost certainly would have spoiled her as a tourist attraction.

The Bermuda those early tourists encountered was in many ways markedly different from today's: naturally there were no motor vehicles (nor were there any anywhere else in the late 1800's); the pace of life was slower; the island was far less crowded (the population at the turn of the century was less than a third of today's); life was, for most, essentially a rural one.

And yet, the vital elements of the "Bermuda experience" which draws the visitor today were already present: the hospitality of the people, the quiet beauty of the island (**opposite**, a view of the Paget shoreline facing Hamilton Harbour) and the charm of the simple, unpretentious architecture Bermudians had fashioned in their island, visible in as prosaic a structure as a rustic gate near Spanish Point (**this page**).

*I*ndeed, many would argue that Bermuda's traditional architecture is its outstanding art form. As with all outstanding architecture, Bermuda's combines beauty with suitability to local materials and conditions: as with old European farm houses, nearly every feature of the Bermuda cottage has its logic, and the result are buildings which seem of a piece with the landscape.

The Bermuda builder began with two basic native materials: limestone and cedar. Seventeenth-century construction of cedar, wattle-and-daub, and palmetto thatch threatened to exhaust the cedar forests and proved too weak to withstand the hurricanes which periodically swept the island; thus from the 18th-Century onward, limestone was the prime building material for walls and roof, with cedar used for structural support, doors and windows, and for interior decoration.* The hurricane danger also demanded low, ground-hugging buildings with narrow eaves. The famous Bermuda "cake-icing" roof itself results from the overlapping of limestone slates, covered with a sealing mortar which is then painted or whitewashed; tapered or "stepped" chimneys economized building material while lending lateral support to the cottage (**upper left, opposite**).

Most building sites were sloped, owing to Bermuda's rolling topography, and Bermudians turned this feature to their advantage by carving a cellar into the hillside, resulting in an impressive two-story front while requiring the building of only one story in the rear (the excavation also provided stone for walls and roof); the tapered steps leading up to the front door were framed in what came to be called "welcoming arms," in reference to Bermuda's tradition of hospitality (**upper right, opposite**).

Because the native limestone is so soft (it was historically quarried, and is still cut, with handsaws), and the climate so damp, it is unsuitable for fine exterior decoration; hence the simple, unadorned lines of the traditional cottage — a plainness which perhaps prompted the frustrated architect to indulge in an occasional, largely decorative "eyebrow" over a door or window (**lower right, opposite**).

A larger home might have a "buttery," a small outbuilding with thick walls and high, steep roof, which served to protect perishables against the heat. Even since the advent of refrigeration, many newer homes feature a storage building in the traditional buttery shape (**lower left, opposite**).

Thus evolved the classic Bermuda cottage, such as Stamp House (**this page**), on the South Shore Road in Warwick Parish (the house dates from about 1705, although the name is a recent one, coming into fashion in the 1960's after the cottage served as the model for a Bermuda postage stamp), one of the oldest cottages in Bermuda still used as a private residence.

As with all Bermuda homes, its white roof doubles as a catchment for rainwater, since the permeability of the subsoil makes fresh-water wells an impossibility. The rainwater is then channeled to a cistern (partially visible at right in the picture). Though their brick-red color is unusual in a land where pastels prevail, the walls of Stamp House, again like those of virtually all limestone cottages, are plastered inside and out—to protect the soft limestone walls.

---

*But each era has its dangers: after three-and-a-half centuries of cutting up the island for building material, Bermudians have come to realize that uncontrolled quarrying, too, presents risks to the island's beauty; today quarrying is carefully controlled, and concrete blocks and roof tiles of synthetic material often take the place of limestone in modern home construction.

A large collection of antique Bermuda and West Indies maps, dating from the 17th to the 19th Centuries, line the wall of the central stair hall (**this page, lower**), through which rises a splendid cedar staircase. The drawing room (**this page, upper**) ("You'll learn that the nicest room in these old houses was invariably called the drawing room," Mrs. George Wardman, Mount Pleasant's owner, informed me with a laugh.) is a treasure-room of antiques, among them a cedar side chair dating from the 1720's, mahogany chairs from the late 18th Century, and a 19th-Century cedar cabinet.

*T*hough the simple cottage sufficed for the average Bermudian household, as some Bermudian fortunes rose—especially as the sea trades came into their own with the 18th Century—so did the desire for grander houses. Perhaps most renowned of those large houses is Mount Pleasant, high on a Paget hilltop overlooking Hamilton Harbour. As with many large Bermuda homes, it has been added to over the years (the wooden porches, seen in the frontal view, **opposite**, date from the 1860's, for example), a tribute to the quality of original construction—as well as to the thriftiness of those Bermudians!

S ome of the sea-faring home-builders pre-ferred houses closer to the water, where the structure could do double service as a residence and for commercial purposes. Thus Spithead (**this page**), built in the late 1700's on a point of land jutting into the Great Sound, served the famous privateer Hezekiah Frith as both home and warehouse. The story is told that Frith discovered the point of land on which Spithead sits to be a strategic location: a ship anchored on its western side was hidden from the view of anyone in Hamilton who might be looking—such as customs officials. (Much later, in the 20th Century, Spithead would have another famous owner: the American playwright Eugene O'Neill.)

No such ulterior motive has been attached to the location of Blackburn Place (**opposite**), just across Harbour Road from Darrell's Wharf on Hamilton Harbour—which suited admirably the needs of 19th-Century sea captain Nathaniel Darrell (who used the ground floor as his warehouse and lived on the second story). Though part of the house dates from 1730, it, too, has been enlarged over the years, the front wings dating from 1820. The huge bay grape tree which shades the front lawn is said to be the largest, and perhaps the oldest, in Bermuda.

*B*loomfield, another Paget Parish home overlooking Hamilton Harbour and the Great Sound, dates from the 1720's. Though grander in their aspect, most larger Bermuda homes nonetheless share many of the traits of the simple Bermuda cottage, from whose tradition they evolved. Thus they tend to complement, rather than clash with, the architectural landscape.

One characteristic common to early Bermuda homes, large or small, is the fact that it was difficult to find cedar logs which could yield beams longer than sixteen feet, which effectively limited the width of rooms, no matter how large the house. The solution in larger homes was often to build in an "E" or "U" pattern (as with Bloomfield) which yielded a larger structure without sacrificing flow-through ventilation.

And a characteristic of nearly all Bermuda homes, old or new, small or large, is the fact that they are named, rather than numbered. Many of the names, like those of Mount Pleasant, Bloomfield, Norwood, Somerset, and Rosemount, to name a few, evoke poetic or historic associations, while some others (I encountered "Wit's End," "Dream Come True," and "Just A Start," for example) reveal a more whimsical bent. Whatever their inspiration, the names of Bermuda's houses add to its storied charm. (And are sometimes the postman's headache!)

. . . and a Few Onions

The appeal of Bermuda, it is often remarked, lies as much with the charm of her people as with her land. Whether it was five-year-old Ranike Dill (**this page**), whom I saw at a church bake sale in St. George, or the mayor of Hamilton, I found a blend of openness, self-assurance, and a lack of pretense which made nearly every encounter a memorable one.

(Perhaps it is here, in fact, that I should remark that the time I spent "covering" Bermuda as a writer-photographer was one of the most pleasurable periods of my life. Having recently experienced another country where a photographer was

regarded with suspicion and often outright distaste, I was in a better position than most to appreciate the Bermudian traits I describe above. If this book seems overly laudatory of Bermuda, it is probably because it is hard to come away from the island with anything but a good feeling for the country.)

I first encountered Sir Henry Tucker in St. George as well, where he had agreed to pose for me in the historic Tucker House (**opposite**), where an earlier generation of the extended Tucker family had made its mark.* Perhaps no other living Bermudian has figured so prominently on the Bermudian scene as has Sir Henry: His public life has included thirty years in the legislature and service as Bermuda's first Government Leader under the 1968 Constitution (the equivalent of the Premier under today's terminology). His private life has been no less impressive: as head of Bermuda's largest bank, he, together with a handful of others, was the moving force in Bermuda's becoming an international corporate, financial, and insurance center. Today the employment provided by over 4000 "exempt" companies (meaning enterprises incorporated in Bermuda, but doing business abroad) is second in importance only to the tourist industry, and constitutes a much-sought diversification of Bermuda's economy.

But the above is only part of his success—many have attained renown and material reward, and in the process gained the enmity of subordinates and the general public. Sir Henry, I discovered, is probably the most widely respected and liked man on the island—and, for me, nothing speaks so eloquently to that than the fact that this knight is known to one and all simply by his nickname, "Jack." ("I have no idea where that came from," he remarked with a laugh, "I got it as a boy, and it just stuck.")

---

*The Henry Tucker for whom the house is named was president of the Governor's Council when the colony was still in its formative years; he and his relatives figured prominently in the island's early history. Unfortunately, no portraits of him are known to exist, but several 18th-Century members of his family, including two other Henry Tuckers—obviously the family has had a fondness for the name—are portrayed on the walls beyond Sir Henry. The house is today a museum, filled with 18th-Century cedar antiques, and administered by the Bermuda National Trust.

Master of an abstract style ("basically French impressionist, with Japanese influences," he explained) which has made him Bermuda's best-known artist ever, Alfred Birdsey works on a watercolor in his studio at Stowe Hill, Paget (**upper left**). Phenomenally successful, his combined sales of oils, watercolors and prints reach the thousands annually.

But while his art may leave much to the imaginative eye of the beholder (**below, left**, "Lower Ferry," one of his most popular prints), his open manner and outspoken views tell you clearly where he stands: I heard opinions on Bermuda's economy, society, politics, and future during our shooting sessions. Like many an artist, Birdsey came to his art in a roundabout way, working for years in a bookstore and training as a watchmaker ("I think everyone should know how to do something with his hands," he counseled.) before turning to his art full time. The loss to the world of books and watches has been Bermuda's gain: for an army of devotees Alfred Birdsey's art captures—and is a living part of—the essence of Bermuda.

Less well-known abroad, sculptor Chesley Trott (**opposite**) has gained fame within the island as the Bermudian who has revived Bermuda cedar as an art form; his sculptures—in both traditional and modern styles—now command prices in the hundreds of dollars.

Throughout her early centuries, Bermudian craftsmen fashioned the close-grained wood into both utilitarian and fine furniture—some antique samples of the latter now command prices which would have purchased the entire cottage that once housed them—exercising a craft that would disappear in an era of mass production.

As a young man Mr. Trott—perhaps inspired by an aunt who was an amateur painter—saw in the cedar the possibility of developing an art form unique to Bermuda. He was none too soon on the scene, for by that time suitable cedar logs were rapidly disappearing: as a result of the devastating blight which struck the cedar stands in the 1940's (see "Bermudiana"), the stricken trees were being burned in Bermuda's fireplaces. Indeed, it is in no small part due to Trott's artistic success (and that of other sculptors, many of whom he has influenced as an art teacher) that Bermuda cedar has come to be recognized as a scarce national resource. Today the Bermudian homeowner carefully examines a log in his woodpile for artistic value before consigning it to the fireplace, and even the simplest handicrafts made of Bermuda cedar command a premium in Hamilton shops.

Quo Fata Ferunt *(Whither the Fates Lead Us)* reads the country's motto. In 1979, the fates led a young woman from St. George, Gina Swainson, abroad to compete in the Miss World contest. Where the fates had led, her charm and beauty prevailed, bringing her the title and crown of Miss World. No Bermudian has ever struck a more popular response: her triumphant return to the island at the end of that year prompted a national holiday and parade through the streets of Hamilton, where thousands of Bermudians displayed their immense and genuine pride in their "home-town" girl's success. An equally enthusiastic welcome awaited her when she returned to lead the Bermuda Day Parade, **(opposite)**, in June of 1980.

Where the fates will lead Bermuda in the coming years is naturally a question of great import to her people. Much will depend on the employment opportunities the country manages to provide to the some 12,000 youngsters now of school age (like Harrington Primary School's Marvin Ford, framed in a rain-blurred bus window, **this page**), who will be joining the labor force over the next two decades.

*D*renched in sweat, heavyweight Clarence Hill **(upper left)** nears the end of a workout in preparation for the 1980 Olympics. (Bermuda subsequently decided not to participate in the Moscow Games.) In 1976 he had become the first—and at this writing, only—athlete to place Bermuda's name in the Olympic record books, when he won a Bronze Medal in Montreal. Like many other young Bermudians I met, he has discovered that his interests and training have led him into a field which Bermuda's small size and limited economy have no place for: in mid-1980 he was planning to move to Britain to persue a professional boxing career. (In fact, so many Bermudians have gone abroad to persue their destinies that one study estimates that over 3500 native-born Bermudians—nearly 8% of the population—emigrated during the 1960's alone.)

One young Bermudian who went abroad to persue a professional education and career, Anson Nash **(lower left)**, soon discovered that his true passion lay with his life-long interest in carpentry and boatbuilding. He returned to the island, soon associating himself with the Bermuda Maritime Museum, where, among other duties, he heads up the Small Craft Restoration Workshop, a program aimed at preserving and rebuilding samples of traditional Bermudian small boat design. He is pictured here with one of the Workshop's outstanding projects, the restoration of a Bermuda fitted dinghy, which, when completed, will be one of only a handful of the craft in existence.

Anson expressed a concern held by many Bermudians I came to know, that of the environmental cost of the island's recent rapid development: "It's gotten to the point where there's hardly any open space left—about the only place to go for a jog or a long walk is along the roads—and there you choke on exhaust fumes. Change has come so fast that we haven't had a chance to consider its effects; now, in many cases, it's too late to go back."

Hamilton

Hamilton

Capital of the colony, Hamilton was incorporated in 1793, at the urging of then-Governor Henry Hamilton; Hamilton is the island's principal port as well as her only city (St. George being classified as a "town"). Principal points of interest include the Bermuda Cathedral (Anglican), City Hall, Sessions House, Front Street, Perot Post Office, Bermuda Library and Historical Society Museum, Cabinet Building and Fort Hamilton.

St. John's Rd.

Cemetery Rd.

Woodlands Rd.

North St.

Ewing St.

Laffan St.

Angle St.

Elliot St.

Court St.

Cedar Ave.

Brunswick Street

Serpentine Rd.

Dundonald St.

Union St.

Richmond Rd.

Victoria Park

Bermuda Cathedral

Happy Valley Rd.

City Hall

Victoria St.

Fort Hamilton

Ave.

Washington Street

Sessions House

Woodbourne

Bermudiana Rd.

Par-la-Ville Rd.

Church St.

Burnaby St.

Post Office

Parliament St.

King St.

Library

Queen St.

Reid St.

Bermudiana Hotel

Perot Post Office

Front Street Shopping Area

Cabinet Office

Front St.

Pitts Bay Rd.

Cenotaph

Visitors' Service Bureau

Princess Hotel

Ferry Terminal

The Cage

Royal Bermuda Yacht Club

Albuoy's Point

Hamilton Harbour

*T*he colony was nearly two centuries old before the city was even founded (in 1793), but Hamilton soon grew, due largely to its prime location, to be Bermuda's commercial and governmental center (the capital being transferred there from St. George in 1815). The capital's concentration of commercial buildings, and the fact that its tiny area (only 177 acres, compared with 341 for St. George) blends with heavily-populated Pembroke Parish which surrounds it, are deceiving, for it has a resident population of only 2000, making it one of the world's smallest capitals.

Though it is a modern urban center (albeit in miniature) and Bermuda's largest population concentration, Hamilton is ironically also where Bermuda's ties as a close-knit community are daily reaffirmed—for it is a rare Bermudian who walks down Reid Street without stopping two or three times to exchange a greeting or catch up on the latest news with a friend.

The widespread use of the motor vehicle since the 1940's has permitted the population to disperse throughout the island (Hamilton, in fact, has lost population over the past two decades, while that of the island as a whole has steadily increased), but Hamilton's importance today is no less than it was pre-automobile: a survey undertaken in 1972 revealed that most of the island's road traffic was bound to or from Hamilton, where resident and tourist are irresistibly drawn (during summer evenings, as **above**, the lights of cruise ships join with those of the city to make for a lyrical sight).

*P*ausing on Reid Street to share a last word with his passengers, a hire carriage driver evokes a scene (**opposite**) reminiscent of a time before Bermuda knew the automobile, and horse-drawn transport was common. The Second World War saw the end of that era, when American military personnel, manning two island bases, utilized motorized transport. After the war the Bermuda legislature, perhaps not foreseeing the eventual consequences of the decision (**lower left**, a not atypical scene on Front Street), narrowly approved the use of cars by the general public.

In spite of limits on automobile size and ownership (only residents are permitted to drive cars, and they are limited to one car per household), the arrival of the car—and later, the ubiquitous cycle—inevitably altered the island's atmosphere (in both senses of the word). Many Bermudians continue to lament the presence of the noisy, smelly beasts (at least those belonging to others), and scarcely a week passes without some criticism of motor vehicles being aired in the local press.

*   *   *

Reid Street honors a notable 19th-Century Governor of Bermuda, William Reid, who, among other accomplishments, greatly encouraged the island's agriculture, pushed for the construction of Gibbs Hill Lighthouse, and founded Bermuda's first public library.

Later, I visited the Canon's home, where members of the Cathedral's Ladies' Guild were busily turning out needle-point for the Cathedral's kneelers. Over the years the Guild has supplied over 300 of the kneelers for the Cathedral (like the ones pictured **this page, lower right**), each with an original design, many inspired by the scriptures. Over the years the kneelers' renown has spread nearly as far as that of the cathedral itself.

Farther down Church Street, the City Hall (**this page, upper left**) dedicated in 1960, incorporates elements of Bermuda cottage architecture into its design and is topped by the Sea Venture weathervane.

A Bermuda-blue sky sets off the Bermuda Cathedral (**opposite**), dating from the 1890's, and built in the Middle English style (a form of neo-Gothic). Seat of the Anglican Bishopric, the cathedral stands on the site of Trinity Church, destroyed by fire in 1884.

The Anglican Church of Bermuda dates from 1973, when its predecessor, the Church of England, was disestablished, perhaps in recognition of the developing trend toward local autonomy in Bermudian affairs. Although it retains the largest number of adherents, and, through its predecessor, claims the longest history of Bermuda's Churches, the Anglican denomination today coexists with more than 25 others on the island.

I visited with the Cathedral's Canon, the Rev. Peter Hartley, one hot summer Sunday after services, as a throng of Bermuda-short-clad worshippers filed out of the Cathedral. "Looks like you're the only one at a disadvantage," I remarked, referring to his ankle-length surplice. "Not at all," he replied with a chuckle, "I've got my bathing suit on underneath this!"

*A youthful grin earns a greeting from a policeman on Reid Street (**opposite**) during the busy Christmas season. (Bermuda's policemen are not seen in their famous summer uniform until after May 24th, traditionally the first day on which Bermuda shorts are worn.) The island's police force follows the British custom of going unarmed; but Bermudians' preference for other types of work—especially in the high-paying tourist industry—means Bermuda must look abroad for a large proportion of its policemen, mainly to Britain and the West Indies.*

Indeed, Bermuda's employment situation is an enviable one, since its major employment problem is a lack of skilled workers (such as nurses, accountants, and secretaries)—unemployment being essentially non-existent. The country fills its skilled needs by recruiting workers from abroad on a temporary permit basis.

Policemen at crosswalks and street corners are an increasingly rare sight, ever since Hamilton yielded to the fact of increased motor traffic and installed its first intersection traffic lights in 1978.

*A miniature reproduction of Front Street's famed "policeman in the birdcage" serves a commercial purpose in a shop window (**this page**), where it promotes a locally-made liqueur.*

Mention Bermuda to the tourist who has been there, and very likely the first image that will come to his mind is Front Street (**these and following pages**), where a panoply of storefronts representing the full range of the rainbow faces Hamilton Harbour (including, **this page, upper**, Calypso, and, **lower**, Trimingham's). It is here that Hamilton's leading shops, with labels known the world over, are located: shoppers browse through Scottish woolens, Irish linens, and English crystal, or perhaps consider purchasing a locally-made gold charm emblematic of Bermuda, such as a miniature longtail or fitted dinghy.

During the tourist season Front Street is aclamor with activity: an unending stream of taxis picking up their passengers, the shouts of carriage drivers directing their horses ("Come back!" you hear, as a driver backs his carriage into a parking space to await the next fare) and package-laden tourists crowding the arcade-covered sidewalk.

A veritable wall of cruise ships disgorge eager tourists directly onto their new mo-peds ("The worst thing you can do is get behind someone who is worse on one of these things than you are," I overheard one chastened novice mo-peder advise her companion.), who jockey for position with wary veterans, including businessmen on their way to the office **(opposite)**.

A pair of Bermudians, clad in that most famous of Bermudian inventions **(this page)**, pause for a chat before Front Street's line of arcades. Perhaps no other facet of Bermuda's "personality" so surprises the visitor as the omnipresence of Bermuda shorts. ("Even the firemen wear Bermudas!" I heard one incredulous visitor say to another.)

The visitor eventually grows accustomed to seeing businessmen on Front Street, policemen, and even the Anglican bishop, so attired, and, if he is sensible, he soon adopts the style for himself. (A personal note: Having lived in the Caribbean, where businessmen routinely wear suits—the long-trousered kind—through sweltering summers, I can only hope that other cultures will soon adopt this most intelligent of Bermudian habits.)

Hamilton takes on a special charm as evening falls over the city. The noise and congestion of daytime traffic all but disappear, for Hamilton "goes to bed early." Quiet streets and passageways, like boutique-lined Chancery Lane, linking Front and Reid Streets (this page) become especially delightful for the pedestrian, and the 19th-Century Sessions House (opposite) assumes a particular beauty against the fading sky.

Bermudiana

Bermudiana (Sisyrinchium bermudiana),
the national flower (blossom about one
inch across; blooms April-May).

*C*ontestant and owner stand inspection before the judge during an all-breeds show held annually in late spring **(opposite)**. *Several dog shows throughout the year draw entrants from the U.S., Canada, and Britain, as well as from Bermuda's own hundreds of dog fanciers.*

Dog lovers are not the only competitors drawn to Bermuda's shores: bridge players flock to international tournaments, while golfers are attracted by events at the island's six 18-hole courses. But perhaps most renowned among Bermuda's competitions are her sailing events, such as the Newport-Bermuda Yacht Race, held in June of even-numbered years, when several thousand racers, friends and family—as well as those simply drawn to the festive atmosphere— descend on the island for the finish and the partying that follows.

A dog lover after his own fashion, architect Peter Leitner takes "Tacsko" along to a tennis game **(this page)**.

*S*ome of the most charming things about Bermuda are little details often overlooked, like the morning glory decorating the lamp of a carriage awaiting a fare on Front Street (**this page**). One of Bermuda's most prolific forms of vegetation, morning glory is seen everywhere along the roadsides, changing hue as the day progresses.

A strand of the vine creeps across a fallen cedar stump lying beside Middle Road in Southampton Parish (**opposite**), a ravaged reminder of the role *Juniperus bermudiana* once played in the history of the island. Since the earliest days of the colony the cedars, which once covered the island, were vital to its development: in the roof beams of cottages, for furniture, and, above all, in the construction of the boats and ships upon which Bermuda's economy depended. So important was the cedar that legislation prohibiting its export and requiring stone construction of houses had been promulgated by the advent of the 18th Century. But even legislation was powerless against the juniper scale, a blight which invaded the island about 1940, soon decimating the forests.

A program of reforestation was begun in 1949 with the fast-growing casuarina, and the diseased, skeletal cedars were felled to make way. Today the scale-scarred stumps line the roadsides, often overlooked by tourists whizzing by on their mo-peds. Only a few scattered healthy cedars remain, giving some hope that the cedar may one day return to its former place on the Bermudian landscape.

In persuit of a gentler art, students at Warwick Academy (**this page, lower right**) sharpen their skills on the violin in a music class, part of a thorough academic and extra-curricular program offered by the school, which seeks to combine elements of both British and North American approaches to education. The Academy boasts an august scholastic tradition dating back to 1662—making it the oldest of Bermuda's schools, and one of the oldest in the Western Hemisphere.

A total of more than 40 institutions, both private and public, compose an educational system guaranteeing free, compulsory education through the secondary level, and have created one of the world's lowest illiteracy rates. A limited program of higher education is available at Bermuda College, but students seeking to attend university must go abroad (most choosing Britain or North America).

Traditional whites, decorum, an almost stately atmosphere—appropriate to a game emanating from Imperial Britain—characterize a cricket match in progress at Southampton Oval (**this page, upper left**). The season finishes up with Cup Match, that annual festivity (held in commemoration of Emancipation Day, August 1, 1834) when the entire island goes half-crazy over cricket.

But if cricket has tradition on its side, it is sometimes rough-and-tumble soccer which seems more in tune with modern tastes. Here (**opposite**) a Devonshire Rec team (in yellow) battles it out with Dandytown under a winter drizzle.

D uring the school year, the Hamilton bus depot is alive with schoolchildren, each in the uniform of his respective school, doing all the things kids have always done between school and home (**this and opposite pages**).

As with children everywhere, Bermuda's are both a joy and the future in the making. About Bermuda's future one thing seems clear: the island cannot afford a much larger population if its quality of life is to remain unaltered. Already, close to 60,000 residents create a population density of over 3000 per square mile (one of the world's highest)—and those figures are over 50% higher than they were in 1950. Such a population density is sometimes hard to reconcile with appearances—the island's rolling topography and heavy vegetation give the impression of sparse settlement; an aerial view of the island, looking east from Gibbs Hill Lighthouse (**lower**), gives a truer picture: white roofs everywhere.

By the 1970's Bermudians had become fully conversant with the problems of overcrowding and the threat it poses to Bermuda. By then strict limits had been imposed on foreigners' employment and property acquisition, as well as on immigration itself; concerned about the maintenance of Bermuda as a quality resort, the government had moved to control new hotel construction and cruise ship visits.

"We could increase our cruise ship calls by perhaps 25%," one tourism official confided, "but what is the value of increasing sheer numbers of visitors if they go away disillusioned with Bermuda? We'll be in this business for a long time to come, and for us there's no better advertising than the visitor who already knows our island." Bermuda's approach to "advertising" seems to be working very well: about 40% of her tourists are "repeaters," a very high figure for the tourist industry.

*L*earning their trade from the kitchen floor up, a class of hotel administrators-to-be at Bermuda College's Department of Hotel Technology prepare a meal (**this page**) in the school's restaurant kitchen.

"As dependent as we are on tourism," the department's head, Martin Barnes, told me, "we can't afford anything but first-class people in our tourist industry. So we teach future administrative personnel how to cook as well as how to manage—how else can they properly supervise a hotel kitchen?" But above all, he continued, "We try to instill an attitude of excellence, a pride in service. It's vital to this business, and, once lost, almost impossible to regain. We plan never to lose it."

(A meal in the school's restaurant later revealed excellent work in the kitchen and eager, if not yet fully polished, attention by the students in the dining room.)

Small wonder that Bermuda tends carefully to her tourist industry: as an island essentially without raw materials or manufacturing, tourism directly accounts for close to 40% of her total employment, and for an even greater share of her prosperity. Thus Bermudians have a very big stake in maintaining the elements that have made their island a "quality tourist destination," to quote the guidebooks.

This is not to suggest that Bermuda is a paradise where no problems exist: the same moped, for example, that is generally seen as a quaint means of transport takes on a different aspect when a "pack" of youthful riders tears around a blind curve with scant regard for the center dividing line. And even Bermuda's roadsides, spanking clean compared to most, are beginning to accumulate the trash of a "throw-away" society. Other problems, involving employment opportunities, educational quality, and housing, to name a few, impinge as well.

But such problems, at least at their present level, are serious only within the Bermudian context: the island is, on the whole, so beautiful and well-run, its population on the whole so prosperous, that any deviation from the ideal tends to assume a magnified import.

Given the pride Bermudians hold in their island, and their concern that it remain one of the truly idyllic places in the world for resident and visitor alike, it is more than probable that visitors will be coming to share a bit of the Bermudians' special world for generations to come.

Three off-duty sailors from a visiting Royal Navy ship find a touch of home in one of Bermuda's pubs as they sample a bit of that famed Bermudian hospitality (**this page**).

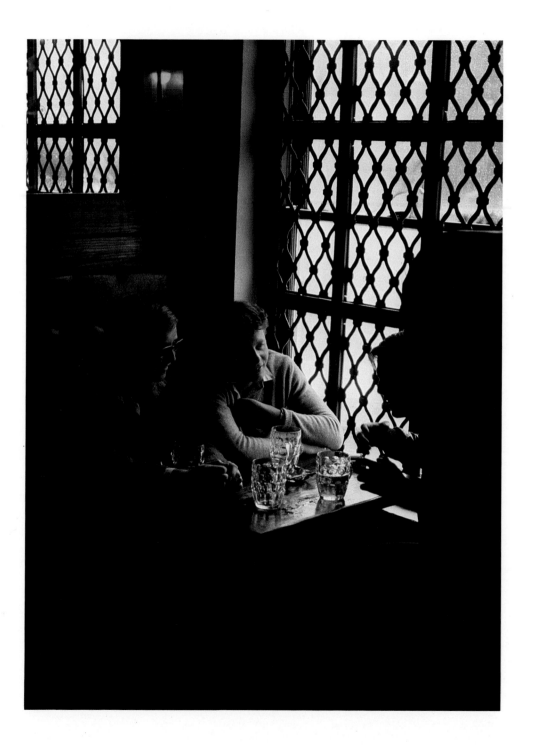

W herever you roam in Bermuda, the roads are bordered by limestone— either a solid wall, where a "cut" has been made through a hill, or by drystone or "slave" walls (after their original builders), composed solely of rough-cut limestone blocks carefully fitted together. Being Bermuda, they are usually graced with the lush vegetation, such as morning glory or nasturtium—or perhaps a mere common thistle—which leads to comparisons with Eden (**upper left**).

Even a paradise has its dissidents, however, and Bermuda's walls, like walls everywhere, are a handy place to express their views. The call for "Africa Now" (**lower left**) is likely the sentiment of a Ras Tafarian (or "Rasta," as they are usually called), a tiny sect with origins in Jamaica whose creed includes rejection of European-based culture and a call for a return to Africa.

And being Bermuda, a way was found to give even a prosaic wall a bit of enchantment. Though often disclaimed as a part of the "true" Bermudian architectural heritage, the moongate (**opposite**) nonetheless speaks of a part of Bermuda's past, when her sloops and sailors roamed the globe, bringing home from the Far East oriental vases which to this day decorate grand Bermudian homes, and bringing home as well an idea for decorating Bermuda's walls. Despite the disclaimers, the moongate has become a romantic part and parcel of Bermuda's landscape.

*T*hroughout her history, Bermuda's position as a strategic British outpost has played a central role. That role came to an end in the post-World War II era, as Britain retrenched, but by then the United States had seen the value of the island for off-shore bases. In 1941 the greater part of St. David's Island was granted to the U.S. (under a rent-free 99-year lease) for construction of an airfield, and throughout the war the island served as an American base of operations.

Today the U.S. Navy's fleet of P-3 Orions (as **upper left,** approaching for a landing against a setting sun) maintains a constant anti-submarine patrol, operating out of the Naval Air Station on St. David's. (The field serves double duty as Bermuda's civil airport.) The base's American staff and their dependents seem well received by Bermuda's people, and bring yet more American culture, such as Little League baseball (**lower,** a game in progress at the base), to the island.

It is hardly surprising that Americans and Bermudians should get along well: they have common interests and family ties dating back to their earliest colonial days, when the Virginia-bound Sea Venture stumbled upon Bermuda. The ties have been maintained and strengthed throughout the years by trade, travel, emigration (in both directions), and inter-marriage.

Endings

For the photographer, Bermuda is a symphony of light, land and water; my favorite time for photographing the island is near sunrise and sunset, when the moods of the island change dramatically within the span of an hour or two.

An early-rising equestrian (**this page**) shares the solitude of Warwick Long Bay with a lone beach stroller on a summer morning. Later in the day sun bathers and swimmers will give the beach a more familiar appearance.

Perhaps no aspect of Bermuda so attracted me as a photographer as the ferry boats which ply Hamilton Harbour on their regular runs between Hamilton and the Paget and Warwick shores. Here (**opposite**), a late-afternoon ferry departs the Salt Kettle landing as the sun fades into the clouds beyond Somerset. Though today carrying fewer commuting residents than in the days before the automobile, the ferries continue to be one of the island's greatest enchantments for the visitor.

In a small glade on Ireland Island, just before the traveller reaches the Dockyard, is the old Naval Cemetery. It's worth a visit, a short walk among the headstones dating from the past two centuries, reminders of the era when Britain was a great sea power, and of Bermuda's role in that era. The headstones recall young men, mostly, ... victims of explosions, disease, drowning* ... headstones of sailors who came to rest far from home.

---

*Accidents of station, rather than battle deaths, for Bermuda has (except for scattered pirate attacks in the 17th and 18th Centuries), throughout its nearly four centuries of settlement, been free of the ravages of invasion and warfare.

A winter moon settles behind Gibbs Hill Light-house, a beacon familiar to mariners and tourists alike. Built in 1848 after years of wrecks and a series of pleas from then-Governor William Reid, the tower was one of the first ever constructed of cast-iron.

Still, its half-million candle power beam has not removed all the hazards of navigating Bermuda's waters: ships continue to go aground on the island's reefs (one as recently as late 1978, when the freighter Mari Boeing grounded on the northern reef).

*A stand of casuarinas on an islet off Somerset Island are silhouetted (**this page**) by the sun bidding farewell to another Bermuda day.*

Sunset colors the North Shore near Bailey's Bay.

. . .and stood entranced, once
before nature's awesome daily
night's beginning, day's end.

Significant Dates

1503-09: generally-accepted period for Bermuda's discovery by the Spaniard Juan Bermúdez (the exact date is uncertain, but it had certainly occurred by 1515).

1515-1609: numerous sailors, mostly Spanish or Portuguese, sight, land on, or are wrecked on Bermuda, thus becoming the first people known to have set foot on the island; 1543 is the date on "Spanish Rock," believed to have been inscribed by one of these Spanish or Portuguese seamen. During this period the Spanish consider establishing a colony on the island, but fail to do so.

1609: the Sea Venture, part of an English fleet bound for Virginia, wrecks on Bermuda's reefs on July 28; after spending ten months there, all but two of the survivors continue on to Virginia. Since Bermuda has been continuously inhabited since this date, it is considered to mark the beginning of Bermuda as a settled place.

1612: having received glowing accounts of Bermuda's commercial potential, the Virginia Company of London receives a charter from King James I to colonize Bermuda as well, and sends out 60 settlers to found a colony. The Town of St. George is founded.

1615-22: Richard Norwood surveys the island, dividing the land into shares, and completes the first detailed map of Bermuda, from which nearly all early maps are derived.

1620: first meeting of the colony's Assembly held in St. George; this marks the beginning of representative government, the earliest in the British Commonwealth outside the British Isles.

1684: the Colony's charter is forfeited by the Bermuda Company (successor to the Virginia Company), and the Colony comes directly under the Crown's administration, although Bermudians retain the right of limited self-government.

1793: City of Hamilton founded.

1810: construction begins on the Royal Navy Dockyard on Ireland Island, which becomes a major naval installation and source of employment for Bermuda until its decommissioning in the 1950's.

1815: transfer of the seat of government from St. George to Hamilton.

1834: emancipation of Bermuda's slaves on August 1.

1861-65: during the American Civil War, Bermuda serves as a base for Confederate blockade runners.

1941: leasing of land for and construction of American bases in Southampton Parish and on St. David's Island.

1946: introduction of motor vehicles for general use for the first time.

1968: April—rioting, primarily racial in origin, occurred after Floral Parade, opening a decade of scattered civil disturbances and strikes. June—first written Constitution comes into effect.

1970: celebration of 350th Anniversary of Bermuda's Parliament.

Acknowledgments

From the experience of having been a reader far longer than a writer, I know that this is a section often overlooked or given short shrift by most readers. It should not be so, at least not with a book of this nature, for it owes a great deal to the cooperation, usually without even a hint of reimbursement, of an untold number of people. Working in Bermuda, as I have mentioned elsewhere, was a great pleasure for me as a photographer, for Bermudians were—nearly unanimously—splendidly helpful in providing access (balconies, rooftops, etc.), and delightfully willing as subjects.

The contribution of many people will be apparent from the text or from the credits at the photographs themselves, but sometimes considerable efforts were expended for material which was eventually not included, and I would be remiss if I failed to say a special thanks to:

Doug Wheeler, as able and willing an assistant as a photographer could ask for
Doug, Andy Miller and Kathy Brem, for their generous hospitality
Charles Webbe of the Bermuda News Bureau, for countless favors and guidance
Sydney Corbett and Gary Phillips, Bermuda Post Office
Mrs. Elizabeth Storey, Anson Nash, and the staff of the Bermuda Maritime Museum
U.S. Navy (U.S. Naval Air Station, Bermuda)
Bermuda National Trust
"Stumpy" Mello
Mayor Norman Roberts and crew of "Venture"
Harry Powell and crew of "Vixen"
Capt. Jan Konig and crew of "Oleander"
"Wink" and Al Kempe
Devon Curtis
Mr. & Mrs. Ford Baxter
George Trott (Crown & Anchor Restaurant)
Warren Hallamore
Emily Fox
Bob Lee
Foxy Cooper
and Martha Hoch and Marie LaBrucherie, for their assistance in the editorial process.

*   *   *

It will be clear to the reader that Images of Bermuda is not an in-depth study of Bermuda's past or present. For the reader wishing a fuller treatment, I would recommend either Terry Tucker's Bermuda, Today and Yesterday, or that splendid work of William E.S. Zuill, Sr., Bermuda Journey: a leisurely guidebook.

Photographic Notes

The photographs for Images of Bermuda *were shot primarily on Agfachrome 64 (Agfachrome 100 was used in some low-light situations), using Nikon equipment (Nikon F2SB, Nikkormat El and FTN bodies, and various Nikkor lenses between 15mm and 500mm in focal length). For underwater photography I used the Nikkormat EL in an Ikelite housing affixed with a dome port.*

Though I feel there are a number of excellent camera systems, for the last 10 years I have used Nikon equipment, for one principal reason: I believe they are unmatched in reliability and ruggedness. One brief incident may suffice to demonstrate that: I had parked my mo-ped in a driveway off Harbour Road one evening to get some shots of a ferry, putting the Nikon F2 in the cycle basket for a moment while I set up my tripod. I heard a crash, turned, and saw that the cycle had fallen against the stone wall, throwing the camera over the wall and down a steep embankment, where it came to rest on a sidewalk. Fearing the worst, I hurried down to inspect the damage—only to find my fears unfounded: there were only some scratches, a small dent, and plenty of dirt to be cleaned off. Body, meter, and lens still functioned perfectly.

Exposure information is not given because it is simply too inconvenient to note it down in most of my shooting. Besides, in most cases the direct through-the-lens meter reading was used; in difficult lighting situations I recommend plenty of bracketed exposures. I took over 5000 photographs in the shooting of Images of Bermuda.

Bermuda (or Somers Islands)

Location and geography: *island group composed of more than 120 islands with a total land area of approximately 21 square miles (53 sq. kilometers), located in the western North Atlantic Ocean (32° 18' N., 64° 45' W.), about 570 nautical miles east of Cape Hatteras, North Carolina, the nearest point of continental land. Bermuda is the exposed tip of an extinct volcano, capped by a layer of aeolian limestone of a generally hilly aspect (maximum elevation, at Town Hill, Smith's Parish: about 260 feet, or 79 meters).*

Population: *(1980, est.) 58,000, most of which is located on the seven principal islands joined by bridges (the population has approximately doubled since 1940); population density among world's highest.*

Government: *British colony, internally self-governing under a written constitution. Crown-appointed Governor responsible for foreign affairs and security matters. Parliament (oldest of British Commonwealth countries outside British Isles, dates from 1620) elected by universal adult suffrage.*

Economy: *based principally on tourism; "exempt" companies (foreign-operating, locally registered) are second-largest employment source. Per capita income one of ten highest in world.*

Climate: *mild, humid, sub-tropical, moderated by Gulf Stream; rainfall distributed fairly evenly throughout year; daytime temperatures in "warm" months (April-November) in mid-70's and 80's F. (20's C.); in "cool" months (December-March), 65-70 F. (low 20's C.).*

Motto: Qua Fata Ferunt *(whither the fates lead us).*

Author-photographer with a few friends: Roger LaBrucherie is a native of El Centro, California; his first two books reported on the Dominican Republic and Barbados.

Grouped around him are students of Mrs. Powell's Nursery School, Friswell's Hill, Devonshire.

(Photograph by Nicole Corbin, age 4, with a little help from the author.)

Atlantic Ocean

ALARM
(Bermudian, 1877)

RAMONA C.
(Bahamian, 1967)

CRISTOBAL COLON
(Spanish, 1936)

ELDA
(American, 1956)

IRISTO
(Norwegian, 1937)

SAN PEDRO
(Spanish, 1594)

AVENGER
(English, 1894)

MARK ANTONIE
(Spanish?, 1777)

NOLA
(Blockade runner, 1863)

CONSTELLATION
(American, 1943)

SEA VENTURE
(English, 1609)

(UNKNOWN)
(Spanish, 1702)

SANTA ANA
(Spanish, 1605)

(UNKNOWN)
(Spanish?, 16th C.)

The Narrows

ST. GEORGE'S I.

St. George

St. George's Harbour

L'HERMINIE
(French, 1838)

ST. GEORGE'S

H.M.S. LORD AMHERST
(English, 1778)

IRELAND I.

Dockyard

BOAZ I.

SOMERSET I.

Somerset

U.S. Naval Air Stn.
(Airport)

ST. DAVID'S I.

St. David's Lighthouse

Bailey's Bay

HAMILTON

SANDYS

Ely's Harbour

Dundonald Channel

Spanish Pt.

Shelly Bay

Harrington Sound

Castle Harbour

Tucker's Town

MUSSEL
(Bermudian, 1926)

Great Sound

PEMBROKE

North Shore Rd.

Flatts

DEVONSHIRE

SMITH'S

H.M.S. CERBERUS
(English, 1783)

KATE
(English, 1878)

Hamilton

Spanish Rock

(UNKNOWN)
(Spanish, 1563)

Little Sound

Hamilton Harbour

SAN ANTONIO
(Spanish, 1621)

Harbour Rd.

Middle Rd.

PAGET

MAIN ISLAND

Bermuda

SOUTHAMPTON

WARWICK

South Rd.

Gibbs Hill Lighthouse

MARY CELESTIA
(Blockade runner, 1864)

VIRGINIA MERCHANT
(English, 1661)

N

DENOTES WRECK

Miles

Kilometers

Notes

There will be those — Terry Tucker will be among them — who will disagree with my designation of the town on St. George's Island as "St. George," rather than "St. George's."

I admit that one more often sees the latter form in print today, but I believe the historical record is at least as supportive of the non-possessive version, and, in the interest of clarity, I have opted for it in designating the town, while using the possessive to designate the parish and island.

* * *

It was brought to my attention just prior to going to press that, contrary to my assertion in "...and a few Onions" a likeness of the historic Henry Tucker does in fact exist. I regret the error.

Special color processing by Color Craft, San Diego

Printed in Hong Kong

ISBN 0-939302-02-0 (Glossy edition)
ISBN 0-939302-04-7 (Deluxe clothbound edition)